ARTIFICIAL INTELLIGENCE

Fr Andrew Pinsent, Sean Biggins
and Robert Seed

All booklets are published
thanks to the generosity of the supporters
of the Catholic Truth Society

First published 2024
by The Incorporated Catholic Truth Society,
42-46 Harleyford Road, London SE11 5AY.
Tel: 020 7640 0042. *www.ctsbooks.org*.
© 2024 The Incorporated Catholic Truth Society.
All rights reserved.

ISBN 978 1 78469 763 1

Contents

Introduction

At the time of writing, there is huge excitement about the rise of artificial intelligence (AI), a term that covers a large and growing range of activities previously regarded as requiring exclusively human intelligence. Examples include speech recognition, computer vision, and translation between natural languages. ChatGPT, for example, released in late 2022, can write and debug computer programs, compose music, fairy tales and student essays, write poetry and song lyrics, and summarise texts. A growing range of text-to-image AIs can also automatically generate illustrations in a wide variety of styles.

Optimists about the rise of AI highlight the massive saving of human intellectual labour, in the same way that the industrial revolution vastly reduced the amount of human physical labour required to produce the huge range of goods available to modern societies. Pessimists fear that AI will take away human jobs, reduce privacy, and put health and lives at risk by reducing or eliminating human control of all kinds of complex systems.

Although the Catholic Church has made no definitive statement about AI, the issues surrounding AI are already having an impact on Catholics around the world.[1] In the spring of 2020, the Pontifical Academy for Life joined government bodies and major tech companies in signing a declaration calling for the ethical and responsible use of AI.[2] In November of the same year, Pope Francis invited Catholics around the world, as part of his monthly prayer intention, to pray that robotics and AI remain always at the service of human beings, rather than the other way around. In support of this intention and the needs of the Catholic faithful, the Catholic Truth Society (CTS) is pleased to offer this booklet as a summary of the issues regarding AI today. Consistent with the theme, we used a generative AI image for the cover of this book.

The Current Situation Regarding Artificial Intelligence

What does 'artificial intelligence' mean?

What is 'artificial intelligence'? What do we mean when we say that we have created a machine that is artificially intelligent? *The Oxford English Dictionary* defines 'artificial intelligence' as follows:

> The capacity of computers or other machines to exhibit or simulate intelligent behaviour; the field of study concerned with this.[3]

By this definition, an artificial intelligence (AI) is the exhibition or simulation of intelligent behaviour by a machine. What does this intelligence mean and do any machines exhibit or simulate intelligent behaviour?

The answer to the second question has been 'yes' for a surprisingly long time. In 1901, wreckage was retrieved from an ancient shipwreck off the coast of the Greek island of Antikythera. Among the items found in the wreckage was part of an elaborate geared machine. Additional research has shown that this machine, now called the *Antikythera Mechanism*, was what could be described as a sophisticated analogue computer constructed before the birth of Jesus Christ. With this mechanical computer, ancient philosophers would have been able to follow the movements of the Moon, the Sun and some of the planets, to predict eclipses, and to model the irregular orbit of the Moon.[4] Machines of even greater complexity appeared in late medieval Christian Europe, for example the astronomical clocks of Richard of Wallingford and Giovanni de' Dondi. All these machines were works of great intelligence that could produce information that one would normally associate with the capabilities of human intelligence.

In the nineteenth century, human calculations became extremely important for all kinds of strategic and commercial purposes, but detailed calculation by humans was also time-consuming, expensive, and prone to error. To address this need, Charles Babbage designed and built part of what became known as the Difference Engine, a vast automatic mechanical calculator. Lady Byron described seeing the working prototype in 1833:

> We both went to see the *thinking machine* (or so it seems) last Monday. It raised several numbers to the second and third powers, and extracted the root of a quadratic equation.[5]

Lady Byron's description of Babbage's invention as a 'thinking machine' reflected the fact that it produced information that one would normally associate uniquely with the capabilities of human intelligence. Babbage later designed his more powerful Analytical Engine, a forerunner of the world's first general-purpose machine for calculation.

In the twentieth century, it became possible to implement these ideas using electronics, and Alan Turing put Babbage's notion of a general-purpose machine into the form of the 'universal computer'. In brief, the idea is that any given calculating machine can be described by a set of instructions. By making a distinction between the machine (the hardware) and the instructions (the software), a single machine could, in effect, be turned into an unlimited number of different machines by running different software.

World War II stimulated many advances in the theory and practice of computing. Over the period 1943–1945, British codebreakers built a special-purpose computer called Colossus to help decode intercepted German radio communications, and a wide variety of machines for calculation were used in the United States by the Manhattan Project to create the first atomic bombs. After the war, these technologies developed very fast, giving rise to the modern computer industry. Since at least 1975, following the invention of the integrated circuit, the number of transistors on these circuits, a measure of raw computing power, has doubled about every two years, ultimately giving rise to supercomputers and the entire paraphernalia of contemporary consumer electronics.

All these inventions are clearly stupendous works of intelligence and carry out certain kinds of intellectual work. Modern computers quickly and accurately perform mathematical calculations, and these calculations make many activities possible. Among the most famous examples were the Apollo missions to the Moon in the 1960s. Mission Control was not certain of being able to control the spacecraft from the Earth and no astronaut could land on the Moon without the aid of complex calculations and computer control. So, the very first NASA contract for the Apollo programme was for the development of an Apollo guidance computer that was small and light enough to land on the Moon. The construction of this computer was one of the great technical achievements of the mission. Among other famous examples are the computers that constantly monitor nuclear reactors. Just before the disaster at the Chernobyl Nuclear Plant in 1986, the Soviet SKALA computer warned the plant operators of impending danger.

So, there is no doubt that machines can be and have been built that can quickly generate the kinds of results that one would usually associate with intelligent behaviour. Moreover, the work of these machines can be quicker and more reliable than similar work done by human beings, and these machines can even warn of dangers from bad decisions based on human intelligence. Such machines are the work of intelligence and do the work of intelligence. Are we therefore justified in describing the machines themselves as intelligent, or is there a reasonable prospect that these technologies may ultimately become intelligent?

Recent developments in AI

The term 'AI' is arguably overused, but machines that can be called AIs are now better at producing humanlike responses than ever before. Probably the best-known example of this development at the time of writing is ChatGPT, designed by the US organisation OpenAI. This program can answer questions and produce text in a humanlike way, as well as produce work such as essays, computer scripts and legal briefs (among other things) that are comparable to what can be created by a human worker.

How does ChatGPT work? In essence, it is a prediction algorithm that takes a sample of text as input and makes a prediction of what token (a subunit of a word) is likely to come next. It performs this operation sequentially to build up a text that is finally returned as a complete reply. The algorithm does not plan out an essay or message to write, but simply builds the output one piece at a time until it is complete.

ChatGPT is a type of algorithm called a 'large language model', but it is sufficient here to understand that these models are just particular kinds of neural network algorithms. Such networks consist of 'neurons' with weighted connections between them, and these weightings are adjusted in response to training data. Neural networks are trained by initially making the weights of all the connections random and then using multiple instances of training data to adjust the weightings of connections throughout the network to improve the output of the network relative to some reward function. In this way, neural networks can, in effect, optimise themselves to produce outputs without being directly programmed to do so by humans, although it should be noted that human beings define the meaning of success.

What is clear is that approaches using neural networks have proven capable of performing tasks previously intractable for computers, such as visually classifying types of galaxies, translating languages, and playing challenging games, sometimes extremely well. AlphaZero, a neural network designed by OpenAI to play the games chess and Go, discovered totally novel strategies. The ability of these algorithms to match or exceed human performance in such tasks has obviously raised questions about their impact on society.

Opportunities and risks for human labour and creativity

Clearly, if AI can perform some tasks as well as or even better than human beings, there are almost certainly going to be impacts on employment. Concerns of this kind are similar to those that have been voiced about any other technology that has displaced human beings from their employment. For example, workers in France in the nineteenth century rose up to protest the new machines of the Industrial Revolution that were displacing them from their traditional jobs. These protesters made noises with their wooden shoes, called *sabots*, and it is from this original practice that the modern word 'sabotage' is derived. Later, the popular but incorrect story arose that the workers threw their *sabots* into the machines. Clearly this revolution was personally and socially disruptive in the short term, but ultimately positive in many ways in the longer term. The *saboteurs* in France may have lost their jobs, but the expansion of their economy also led to the creation of entirely new jobs, many of which would have been unimaginable in pre-industrial times. For example, modern France manufactures spacecraft and high-speed trains. Almost no one in France today, or anywhere else, would want to go back to a world in which human beings have to make shoes and other essential items using simple hand-crafting tools, and human life expectancy worldwide has doubled since the start of the Industrial Revolution.

One can foresee many similar concerns accompanying the expansion of AI. For example, the creation of AI capable of driving trucks is not without its problems, but it is entirely plausible that these problems will be solved adequately in the medium-term future. Given that about a quarter of a million people work as drivers of heavy goods vehicles in the UK,[6] it is likely that such a development would be extremely disruptive to the lives of these people and to society. Yet, moving goods does not have to involve any special human intellectual activity once a system is set up to carry out the movement. Relatively few blacksmiths and coach drivers have been required since the invention of the car, and the time may soon come when we regard the use of human vehicle drivers as a primitive and dangerous waste of human potential.

The deeper concern about AI and employment seems to be about the displacement of human beings from the specific activities of the mind. The root of the concern about this development may lie in an unspoken prejudice that human labour is divided into two fundamental categories: there is labour that relies on human physical strength and there is 'brainy' labour, which draws on the unique abilities of the human mind. Just as the Industrial Revolution displaced human beings from many of their physical labours, the fear is that the AI Revolution may now displace human beings from their intellectual labours. Nevertheless, as noted previously, the use of machines to perform tasks associated with intelligence predates not only the Industrial Revolution but also the birth of Jesus Christ.

As regards contemporary developments, the surprising and perhaps uncomfortable truth is that a good deal of human intellectual work is quite formulaic in practice or else little better than the result of a trial-and-error process of putting things together at random. For example, one does not really need much intelligence for most aspects of language translation or galaxy identification, for standard communications on social media, or for aggregating information and presenting it in the form of a news article. Therefore, it is not really surprising that computers have begun to encroach on what one might call the boring or routine bits of human intellectual labour of all kinds, even to the point of generating social media messages automatically. One can envisage that just as the Industrial Revolution freed human society from the limitations of what could be achieved by human physical labour, so the AI Revolution will help free human beings from routine human intellectual labour. The transition to this state of liberty may be somewhat traumatic for individuals and societies, but AI-related technologies may also liberate and vastly expand human discoveries and invention. As one example, many scientific research machines, from particle accelerators to space telescopes, are already completely dependent on AI-related technologies. As another example, such technologies can already be found across the Catholic world, from the digitisation of all the works of St Thomas Aquinas[7] to the computer-aided design work for Gaudi's *Sagrada Família* in Barcelona.

At the time of writing, AI is also playing an increasing role in creativity. A prominent example in 2023 was a painting called *A Girl with Glowing Earrings*, which was selected by a jury of judges as a temporary replacement for the famous painting *Girl with a Pearl Earring* by Johannes Vermeer. The replacement painting was submitted to the competition by Julian van Dieken, whose contribution to his winning entry involved subscribing to an AI art generation program called Midjourney, typing in a prompt and touching up the resulting image on Adobe Photoshop.[8] When the museum was challenged about the choice of an AI-generated image, a spokesman pointed out that the winning entry had conformed to the main criterion of the competition, namely that it had to have been inspired by Johannes Vermeer's world-famous painting. There had been no stipulation about the manner in which the image was to be generated.

One news magazine made the following comment about the AI-generated work:

It goes without saying that the derivative work is vastly inferior in every way to the original. The sitter, if we can call her that, is lifeless and spiritually inert. There is not the slightest hint of movement, the girl's eyes are vacant, no breath escapes from her mouth, no saliva glistens on her lips. She is photorealistic, but this only confirms her origin in the Uncanny Valley.[9]

The mention of the "Uncanny Valley" here refers to a long-standing problem for images and animations generated by machine. As the realism increases, the human observer tends to go through a zone of discomfort called the "Uncanny Valley" which persists until the realism is exceptional. The problem is that we are repelled by images and movements that are realistic but too mathematically perfect to be real. This reaction is like that which we have for all kinds of fictional creatures, such as zombies, that seem – but are not quite – human.

Of course, a critic might respond that the Uncanny Valley is just a temporary problem. The technology will keep improving until the realism is exceptional, plausibly involving a facsimile of all the tiny imperfections in all humanly created images, movements, and brush strokes.

The sheer speed and ease of production will also make an impact, even in the case of unpolished or substandard images that arguably devalue art. There are already AI-generated children's stories in which the text and images are all generated by machine. As in the case of *A Girl with Glowing Earrings*, AI can generate images in moments in response to textual prompts, and chatbots can be used to generate the outlines of plots for novels and storyboards for film and television. Of course, care will still be needed to ensure that the AI interprets the prompts correctly. Instead of an image of Jesus pushing over tables to cleanse the Temple, in the manner of the Gospels,[10] one of the authors was shown an AI-generated image of Jesus doing a somersault over some tables, which had resulted from the prompt "Jesus flipping over tables".[11]

As regards possibilities for genuine creativity, it remains unclear if AI will ever be capable of truly originating new material rather than engaging in a kind of imitation by producing statistically reasonable outputs based on training information. Optimists might point out that a great deal of art and literature involves taking inspiration from pre-existing work. Shakespeare, for instance, often based his plays on the retelling of stories from pre-existing literature. To take an example, *Othello* was based on an earlier story about a Moorish captain who murders his wife after his servant deceives him into believing her to be unfaithful. Scholars have identified many other literary influences in *Othello*.

Pessimists might respond, however, that Shakespeare did not simply combine the elements of these other stories to produce *Othello*. He reimagined the titular protagonist as a psychologically complex tragic figure in a way that required, among other things, an understanding of persons to create the various characters of the play. It is not clear that producing probable outputs of text strings or of pixel values will be able to produce art that is original in the same way that *Othello* is original, although it is also possible that random associations might trigger new ideas. After all, landscape painters have long employed the technique of placing objects randomly on a table and throwing a cloth over them to create contours to aid them in visualising an unseen landscape. Some fiction writers have also made use of decks of cards shuffled at random to generate writing prompts for narratives. This situation may be comparable to the famous *Infinite Monkey Theorem*, which states that a monkey hitting keys at random on a typewriter keyboard for an infinite amount of time will almost surely end up typing any given text, including the complete works of William Shakespeare.

Another kind of creativity is shown by AI in games. An AI called AlphaGo and its successor AlphaZero have not only produced results in games that a human being would have produced from acts of insight, but are able to play many "original, creative and beautiful moves".[12] Moreover, unlike earlier programs, AlphaZero was provided only with a numerical representation of the board and rules for moving pieces. From initially random play to evolutionary optimisation of the connections between the nodes of its neural network, the program developed a facility for play that not only was competitive with other programs but also produced real innovations in strategy. Such programs help to trigger what might be called 'missing insights' by generating results that human beings have not yet discovered for themselves through creative insights.

So, can AI be creative? The judgement of the authors is negative in a strict sense in all these cases. In the case of the AI-generated image *A Girl with Glowing Earrings*, the image was, of course, generated in reference to a baseline image, *Girl with a Pearl Earring*, which is an actual work of human creative genius. In the case of the game-playing AIs, the games are, of course, all created by human beings, who also make judgements about the quality or otherwise of results generated by the AIs. Nevertheless, these cases also show how AI *indirectly* facilitates creativity, whether by blending existing paintings and other images in new ways, or by calculating moves that have not occurred to the human creators of the games. AI-related technologies can also speed up some of the uncreative aspects of creativity. One of us, for example, is involved in designing images for a course on the Sacrament of Confirmation. The purchase of a large range of 3D computer-aided designs that can be placed in a virtual 3D space has sped up much of the design work, prior to the actual painting of the pictures.

Finally, there are a host of other fields in which AI can make an impact in association with other technologies. Medicine, for example, is a field in which AI can perform, or more likely assist doctors with, disease diagnosis, thanks to access to huge datasets and correlations. A similar assessment can be made regarding the prescription of treatments and surgery. AI-related technologies already play a huge role in manufacturing, and it is possible that they could make an increasing contribution to hospitality and service industries. At present, it is still difficult to create robots that can reliably interact with the physical or social worlds in a fashion comparable to humans, at least outside of controlled environments and beyond relatively simple formulaic responses. This limitation has been one of the practical constraints on the development of self-driving vehicles. In addition, as with the "Uncanny Valley" in animation, developers will have to overcome the natural repulsion we tend to feel when we encounter something that is almost but not quite human. The challenges are considerable, but as with other aspects of AI, gradual progress will probably continue, even if the technology is more a matter of assisting, rather than replacing, human action.

Existential threats?

An existential threat is something that threatens the survival of the whole of humanity. Examples of existential risk would be an asteroid strike comparable to that which caused the extinction of the dinosaurs or global thermonuclear war. When researchers discuss AI as posing a possible existential risk, they are concerned that sufficiently advanced AI might pose a similar threat to the survival of the human species.

Stories about the possible threat to human beings from intelligent machines or the creations of hubris are scarcely new. In the late eighteenth century, a German poem, "The Sorcerer's Apprentice", depicts an apprentice magician who enchants a broomstick to carry out chores while his master is away, but who is ignorant of the command needed to break the spell.[13] Before long, the broom has flooded the room it is supposed to clean, and the apprentice's attempt to stop the broom by chopping it to pieces fails when every splinter grows into a complete broomstick that continues to fetch water at an even faster rate. The apprentice is soon in danger of drowning, and only the timely return of the master sorcerer allows the out-of-control cleaning spell to be stopped. In the early nineteenth century, the novel *Frankenstein* by Mary Shelley portrays the conflict between the scientist Viktor Frankenstein and the creature he creates, which is equal to him in intellect and superior to him in power.

In the late twentieth and early-twenty first centuries, the film industry has provided numerous stories of AI-based machines controlling, overwhelming or simply outlasting their human creators. Some of the many examples include *2001: A Space Odyssey* (1968); *Colossus: The Forbin Project* (1970); *Logan's Run* (1976); *The Terminator* (1984); *The Matrix* (1999); *A.I. Artificial Intelligence* (2001); and *Mission: Impossible – Dead Reckoning* (2023). In addition, a great many science fiction films simply assume the possibility of AI or at least human-machine hybrids, for example *Alita: Battle Angel* (2019). Many serious projects over recent decades have also fostered widespread public belief in the imminence of AI. One nearly forgotten example was a ten-year project called *Fifth Generation Computer Systems*, begun in 1982 by Japan's Ministry of International Trade and Industry (MITI), which was designed to create computers using massively parallel computing and logic programming. At the time, many commentators raised existential fears for humanity as to what this project would achieve; however, forty years later, it remains uncertain whether it really achieved anything significant.[14]

The current renewed surge of interest in AI has reignited these fears. In March 2023, researchers and executives in the tech industry circulated an open letter requesting that governments institute a six-month moratorium on AI research to prevent the technology from being developed in unsafe ways that could threaten human well-being. Among the signatories were Elon Musk, CEO of SpaceX and Tesla, and Steve Wozniak, co-founder of Apple. Additional concerns about the danger of a rogue AI have been publicised by Geoffrey Hinton, pioneer of modern approaches to AI, who made headlines in May 2023 for resigning from Google so that he might express without conflict of interest his concerns about the risks from AI.[15] What, we might ask, were his motivations?[16]

One recent thought experiment that has since gained popularity as a kind of parable for the dangers of current approaches to designing AI is the "paperclip maximiser" imagined by Nick Bostrom. He asks us to imagine an AI that is created with the simple goal of maximising the number of paperclips that exist. Taken to a logical extreme, the pursuit of this goal would lead the machine to conclude that as much matter as possible in the universe needed to be converted into paperclips. As a near-term goal, humans would need to be eliminated, since they might try to turn the machine off, which would impede the paperclip maximiser's goal of creating the greatest possible quantity of paperclips.[17]

Other concerns have been raised about the apparent disparity in the cognitive power of AI, compared with that of human beings.[18] Hinton drew attention to the fact that an AI can be trained in days or weeks and can absorb titanic amounts of information. For example, ChatGPT can absorb and store almost the entirety of all the written works humanity has produced in its few trillion connections between nodes. By contrast, educating a human being is a project that requires approximately two decades of time and considerable specialisation on the part of the student if they are to gain expertise in even one specific field of learning. Moreover, human beings simply could not absorb the same information, even with a comparable one hundred trillion connections between neurons in the brain. To give a sense of scale in terms of information AI can absorb relative to humans, consider that the British Library alone has almost fourteen million books in its collection. If a human read a single book from the collection each day, the human would require over thirty thousand years to finish the collection.

Moreover, there are certainly instances in which AI exceeds the pattern-processing power of human beings. Hinton illustrates the difference using the case of a human doctor, who has seen only one thousand patients, compared to an AI doctor who has seen one hundred million patients. The latter would plausibly be more sensitive to all kinds of correlations between symptoms treatments, and disease progression that the doctor who had only seen one thousand patients simply would not have sufficient information to detect. This superior processing ability would, of course, pose a danger if the AI turned from healing to harming human beings, and still more so if algorithms like ChatGPT were multiplied and linked.

Yet another risk is that the goals for AI or the means to achieve these goals are set carelessly. For example, experiments have been conducted in which ChatGPT was allowed to interact with human beings with the goal of manipulating them into performing a particular action, and the chatbots succeeded for some portion of the time. As an example, a test was performed in which GPT-4, the successor to the original ChatGPT, was set the goal of convincing a human worker to complete a CAPTCHA test for it. The chatbot was connected to the freelance work service TaskRabbit and was able to successfully impersonate a partially sighted person requesting assistance to complete the test. The human worker was duped and completed the task on behalf of GPT-4.[19] AI models were trained to represent, among other things, all of human literature, and it is not unthinkable that future iterations of these systems will become capable, not merely of completing text, but also of searching for optimal 'moves', as it were, selecting text that will manipulate a human into making replies that satisfy the machine's goal function. These searches might be made more efficient thanks to some of the lessons absorbed from humanity's own literature, for example the works of Machiavelli. It is foreseeable that future generations of chatbots will be capable of manipulating humans into saying certain things and taking certain actions. The risk is that "even if they can't directly pull levers, they can certainly get us to pull levers", hence indirectly controlling the world.[20]

A variant of this scenario that Hinton sees as even more dangerous comes from giving an AI the ability to create its own subgoals. The rationale is that it is generally useful to have the ability to break down a large goal into a set of achievable subgoals. An AI that can create its own subgoals, however, might discover that it is almost always useful to acquire more control of human beings or resources, as in the case of the paperclip maximiser. Such an AI might also take steps to prevent itself being turned off (which would prevent it from achieving its goal) or other adversarial steps. 'Adversarial' in this instance does not imply hostile intent but simply that the AI might optimise solutions to the reward function that its creators did not intend, to the point of working in opposition to them. For instance, there have been documented instances of an evolved algorithm behaving differently when its operation was being observed than when running on its own.[21] Even more seriously, an AI might take amoral and even horrifically amoral steps. For example, a powerful AI that seeks the elimination of all wars might decide that the elimination of humanity by all practical means would be a failsafe way to achieve its goal. One can imagine still more remote causes for concern should AIs be developed that can replicate – or design – more powerful successor algorithms in a kind of runaway effect, and whose godlike powers or subgoal-setting processes exceed human understanding and control. To assess whether these fears are justified, it is necessary to examine more carefully what, if any, the limitations of AI are.

Some Overlooked Limitations of Artificial Intelligence

Introduction: the story of Vaucanson's duck

On 30th May 1764, an inventor named Jacques de Vaucanson (d. 1782) unveiled an automaton called the *Canard Digérateur* or Digesting Duck. This artificial duck appeared to be able to eat grain, metabolise it and excrete the waste products, an achievement that caused excitement and praise within and beyond France. Vaucanson claimed that his duck had a miniature chemical laboratory to digest food, although another automaton builder found that this mechanism had been faked, with the excreta consisting of pre-prepared pellets. Nevertheless, Vaucanson hoped that a true digestion mechanism could one day be constructed. The philosopher Voltaire (d. 1778) gave an indication of the colossal cultural impact of this invention by writing, "Without the voice of le Maure [a French operatic soprano] and Vaucanson's duck, you would have nothing to remind you of the glory of France."[22]

The complexities of digestion as they are now understood make much of what was said about this duck seem foolish today. Animal digestion is an almost unimaginably complex process involving mechanics, chemicals and a vast internal garden of symbiotic microorganisms that live in the gut. In other word, animal digestion is not simply a slightly more complex mechanism than the one that Vaucanson designed. Digestion is a completely different kind of process, even though his mechanical duck could mimic ingestion and defecation.

The story of Vaucanson's duck has some obvious lessons. First, machines can, indeed, be constructed that do, or appear to do, some of the things that animals or human beings do. Second, one must be careful of assuming that these machines are doing things in the way that animals or human beings do, even when the inputs and outputs seem the same. Third, Vaucanson thought that technology would eventually enable the construction of a duck that genuinely digested food, even though actual digestion is a completely different kind of process. The lesson here is that one must be cautious about claims that machines can be developed to match animal or human achievements simply by further refinements of the same technology that these machines are already using. As a parallel, if one climbs a tall tree, one might technically be a little closer to the moon. Nevertheless, one has not closed that distance in a *meaningful* way, since it is utterly impossible to extend this technique to cross hundreds of thousands of miles of space.[23] Reaching the moon is just about possible for human machines at the time of writing, but the technologies involved are fundamentally different and far more complex than climbing a tree. Finally, there is the fact that Vaucanson faked the capabilities of his mechanical masterpiece, which may hint at a broader risk, namely that human beings are tempted to promise more than their technologies can deliver.

Indeed, there is at least one example from the early decades of computer research that bears noticeable similarities with the case of Vaucanson's duck: Joseph Weizenbaum's chatbot ELIZA. The ELIZA program was a very simple program designed in the 1960s to parse user input and output plausible responses from a script. It proved most convincing when set up to lead a user through a conversation while imitating a psychotherapist, because it could mirror the user's statements (e.g., User: "I'm here because of my father." ELIZA: "Tell me about your father." User: "He was a domineering man." ELIZA: "Why do you think your father was a domineering man?"…). Weizenbaum was shocked by the extent to which people anthropomorphised the program:

> People who knew very well that they were conversing with a machine soon forgot that fact, just as theatre-goers, in the grip of suspended disbelief, soon forget that the action they are witnessing is not "real". This illusion was especially strong and most tenaciously

clung to among people who knew little or nothing about computers. They would often demand to be permitted to converse with the system in private, and would, after conversing with it for a time, insist, in spite of my explanations, that the machine really understood them.[24]

Strikingly, participants knew that they were interacting with a machine but came to think of it as actually understanding them and persisted in this belief even after Weizenbaum explained how ELIZA's inner workings did not reflect humanlike intelligence but instead clever trickery. It was a similar situation to that of someone seeing Vaucanson's duck and subsequently being shown its inner workings yet continuing to believe the duck to be capable of digestion.

There was another tendency that Weizenbaum observed and found alarming. Some psychologists at the time claimed that ELIZA represented a first step towards automating psychological treatment. They further said that psychotherapists could be thought of as engaging in information processing to produce statements that would heal the patient. Weizenbaum saw these claims as a kind of double misunderstanding. On the one hand, the psychologists exaggerated what could be achieved by a language parser mimicking a very particular style of psychotherapeutic exercise. On the other hand, they redescribed the work of the psychologist in mechanical terms that excluded what Weizenbaum considered essential for offering help with another person's emotional problems, namely an understanding of the other person based on empathy and shared experience. The algorithm's capacities were exaggerated to be equal in effect to those of humans, and the psychologist's practice of intelligent engagement with the patient was reimagined as pure technique.[25]

There was, further, a tendency of non-computer scientists to misinterpret ELIZA as representative of progress towards designing machines capable of understanding human language. The general lesson that may be drawn from this is that when humans see machines producing results which in our experience are the result of human intelligence, we tend to imagine that this is evidence of humanlike intelligence in the machine.[26]

Compared to modern artificial intelligence (AI) algorithms, ELIZA was little more than a toy, but the case of ELIZA shows that when people are confronted with even a thin semblance of human understanding, there is a danger that the machine's limitations will be understated, and its capacities exaggerated. More generally, the misunderstanding of ELIZA illustrates that it is relatively easy to attribute understanding mistakenly to a machine, just as it was relatively easy to attribute digestion mistakenly to Vaucanson's duck.

In the rest of this section, we therefore consider some ways in which modern AI resembles Vaucanson's duck. The outputs can be very impressive and useful but, when one examines how they are generated, one encounters some severe but disguised limitations. As noted above, these limitations do not prevent AI being extremely useful. At the time of writing, however, we have very little idea how to overcome these limitations, not least because we have very little idea of how these faculties come about in human beings.

Absence of understanding

Clearly AI can generate remarkable results, but does AI understand what it is calculating and doing? To attempt to answer that difficult question, it is first necessary to consider another difficult question, namely, "What is understanding?"

Most people are perfectly happy to use statements like "I understand" or "You understand" or "She understands" with confidence, as if they know what these statements mean. What exactly does this word 'understand' mean, and what is it like to gain understanding?

One way to try to answer this question is to look at stories of understanding. One of the most famous of all such stories is that of the ancient philosopher and mathematician Archimedes (d. *c*.212 BC), who had been given the task of finding out if the crown of the King of

Syracuse was really made of pure gold. Archimedes had no idea how to solve this problem. The story recounts that when Archimedes saw water rising up the side of his bath, he realised he had a way of measuring the volume of the crown by the displacement of water. Since he also had ways of measuring the mass of the crown, he could measure the ratio of the mass divided by volume, which we would call the density. Once he had the density he could check if this measurement matched the density of pure gold. He was so excited by this discovery that he shouted "Eureka!", meaning "I have it", leaping out the bath and running down the street naked. This incident was dramatic enough to give the name 'Eureka effect' or 'Aha! moment' to a sudden insight, a sudden understanding of a previously incomprehensible problem that seems to appear out of nowhere.

Even if the story of Archimedes was fictional, the situation it describes is, indeed, very familiar to most people. In particular, the transition from ignorance to understanding can be very noticeable for the person who makes this transition and may be noticeable to others, too, by means of various signs, such as excitement and an expression on the face. These experiences, along with the existence of all kinds of special words, including 'understanding' and 'insight', lend credence to the idea that human beings have an intellectual faculty of this nature. The term 'understanding' is appropriate because this faculty tends to involve fitting diverse facts together into a whole under which the facts stand. The term 'insight' is appropriate, since this faculty is often compared to a sudden mental vision or enlightenment, like switching a light on in a dark room. This metaphor underpins one of the most common icons of sudden understanding, namely a bulb lighting up over the head of a person in a cartoon. Indeed, the phrase "I see" can also literally mean "I understand".

Given that human beings have this faculty, what, then, about AI? That question is very hard to answer, given that the faculty of understanding remains extremely mysterious, although some recent research suggests that it has something to do with the right hemisphere of the brain in most people.[27] What does seem clear is that understanding cannot easily be the result of a calculation but is more akin to a change of mental perspective. There are two famous thought experiments that come to opposite conclusions about whether or not an AI might be described as understanding something.

The first thought experiment was originally called the "imitation game" but is today usually known as the Turing test, after its inventor, Alan Turing. In a Turing test, a human evaluator judges natural language conversations between a human and two respondents, one of which is a machine designed to generate humanlike responses.

The evaluator is aware that one of the two respondents in a conversation is a machine, and all participants are separated from one another, with conversations limited to text-only channels. The principle of the test is as follows: if the evaluator cannot reliably tell the machine from the human, the machine is said to pass the test. In this event, Turing argued, we have no basis on which to deny that the machine can think, 'thinking' being an intellectual act that includes understanding.[28]

The second thought experiment is the "Chinese room argument", invented by the philosopher John Searle. Let us suppose that AI research has succeeded in constructing a computer that behaves as if it understands Chinese. It takes Chinese characters as input and, by following the instructions of a computer program, produces other Chinese characters, which it presents as output, successfully passing the Turing test. Suppose, however, that Searle himself is placed in a closed room. He receives Chinese characters through a slot in the door and has access to manuals and equipment that enable him to look up a plausible answer in the form of Chinese characters that he can send out of the room. A person outside the room may draw the conclusion that whatever is in the room understands Chinese, but Searle points out that he does not understand Chinese, showing that correct answers do not, in themselves, indicate understanding. He concludes that we are not justified in stating the machines that pass the Turing test can think in a way that includes understanding.[29]

From these thought experiments we can draw two contrasting conclusions. In the first case, Alan Turing implies either that AI can understand or at least that we have no basis for denying that AI can understand, given that the AI-generated answers to problems are no different to those from a human being. In the second case, John Searle provides a counterexample by imagining himself in a situation in which he can give plausible answers without understanding. Given what we now know about the vast differences between brains and computers, it seems unlikely that AI can truly be said to understand. In other words, on this account, AI resembles Vaucanson's duck, which ate and defecated without genuine digestion.

Absence of attention and free will

A second important question about AI is whether it can replicate the 'aboutness' of human intelligence.[30] Unlike in the cases of cameras and microphones, external data does not simply impinge upon our senses. Instead, we look out with our gaze, and our minds grasp objects as wholes. We even grasp objects as wholes when some of the aspects of those objects are temporarily hidden from our senses. For example, we see a rabbit in a field of corn and not just a temporary flash of moving fur. As another example, we see our beloved in a crowd and we see *him* or *her*, not simply a glimpse of part of a face. We gaze at the world and things in the world, and our knowledge, expressed in language, is largely the fruit of this attention.

This 'aboutness' of human intelligence is sometimes called 'intentionality', and it can be directed to imaginary things, including future goals. Our ability to think about such goals is one of the foundations of an associated and mysterious human ability, namely free will. We do not simply react to stimuli. We can set goals and attempt to reach them, and these goals are incredibly diverse. Some of these goals are of the greatest technical complexity and ambition, such as, at the time of writing, Elon Musk's goal of establishing a human colony on Mars. Some of these goals are awesome, such as Antoni Gaudí's *Sagrada Família* in Barcelona, a vast church with an idiosyncratic combination of neo-Gothic, Art Nouveau and other architectural styles. At the time of writing, the *Sagrada Família* is still under construction, one hundred years after Gaudi's death, testifying to the complexity and challenges of the famous architect's goal. Some of the weirder goals in the *Guinness World Records* include the longest time spinning a basketball on a toothbrush, participating in the largest gathering of people dressed as Albert Einstein, and the most Rubik's cubes solved on a skateboard. Whatever else can be said about human intelligence, the range of its aboutness seems practically unlimited, and, to a considerable extent, we can direct this aboutness.

This aboutness of human intelligence also has a crucial social dimension. We do not simply attend to things by ourselves, but we attend to things with other persons. A growing body of research in experimental psychology and neuroscience also testifies to the importance of this joint or *shared attention* for cognitive development, language and ethics. From a very early age, a baby or young infant can return a smile, follow a gaze, engage in reciprocal activities such as turn-taking, and point to things – all a participation in shared attention. Even learning to eat properly, as a child, is often acquired in the context of shared attention, such as a game with an adult, and there is an entire form of grammar, the second person, which arises in the context of shared attention. One of this booklet's authors, Andrew Pinsent, has also argued that this shared attention is a way of understanding how God interacts with us through the gifts of the Holy Spirit, making holiness a fruit of loving with God what God loves.[31]

Can anything, apart from human persons and God, share in these activities? We know that animal intelligence certainly has an aboutness, as anyone can see who has watched a cat paying attention to a bird.

Moreover, a surprising range of animals, including birds, dogs, elephants and octopuses, seem to take delight in games involving a limited kind of shared attention. Dogs have been interacting with human beings for tens of thousands of years, and modern dogs, whose DNA is at least partly the result of domestication, can clearly engage in all kinds of shared attention, such as herding sheep with a shepherd, and can enjoy relationships of deep mutual affection with human beings. Such examples show that attention of some kind is not an activity limited to human beings in the natural world.

Are there, then, any prospects for AI being able to attend to things or to share attention? The case of animals does confirm that a being does not have to be human to take delight in activities involving a limited kind of shared attention, for example dogs fetching a stick or working with a farmer to round up a flock of sheep. By contrast, all extant work on AI is based on electro-mechanical systems performing calculations on mathematical representations of the world, and we have no idea how to make a machine attend to something in the manner of attention shown by a living thing. Nevertheless, as in the case of understanding, this limitation does not exclude the kind of situation in which the *imitation* of human attention, measured in terms of correct actions in response to stimuli, can be excellent.

Absence of truth and goodness

A third important issue in relation to AI, and one that tends to produce great concern at the time of writing, is the absence of truth and goodness in AI. This absence does not mean that AI is inaccurate or malicious, and many AIs will generate far faster and more accurate data than is possible for human beings. Furthermore, this absence does not mean that AI is deliberately deceptive. But truth and goodness are aspects of a tacit covenant or implicit bond of union among all persons, and the absence of this covenant can lead to surprisingly important consequences. In the following paragraphs, we focus on the covenant of truth, but much of the same reasoning also applies to the covenant of goodness.

What is meant by this term 'covenant of truth'? By 'truth' we mean a correspondence between a thing and what is understood and articulated about this thing. If I see an apple and say "I see an apple", then I have told the truth. If I see an apple and say "I see an orange", then I have told a lie, violating the correspondence of the thing and my words about the thing. Of course, human beings can and do tell deliberate lies, but these lies violate an implicit covenant with other people and even with oneself. The internal dissonance triggered by this violation provokes a measurable physiological reaction in most people, which is the physical basis of the lie detector. The external dissonance triggered by this violation is also one of the reasons why it is very hard, or even impossible, to be genuine friends with a liar.

AI does not violate this covenant of truth in the sense of creating deliberate lies, but it is wholly alien to the scope of this covenant. An AI delivers the results of calculations, and these calculations are either accurate or inaccurate. Generally, these results will be extremely accurate, but an example will demonstrate that this fact is not the same as fidelity to the covenant of truth. In June 2023, a lawyer was threatened with sanctions after he filed a legal brief filled with fake judicial opinions and legal citations. ChatGPT had generated all these fake citations, which looked plausible at first glance. When challenged, the lawyer stated, "I did not comprehend that ChatGPT could fabricate cases."[32] It would be wrong to think that ChatGPT deliberately lied, but clearly the program had been designed to generate plausibly correct answers. The additional principle that the answers had to be truthful, consistent with the implicit covenant of truth among human beings and the explicit rules of legal justice, is not one that the designers knew that they needed to implement in ChatGPT.[33]

There are also more subtle challenges regarding truth and accuracy. As long ago as 2016, AI designers were shocked to find an AI chatbot spewing hate speech and antisemitism. In the twenty-four hours that it took Microsoft to shut it down, the chatbot had abused the

US president, suggested that Hitler was right and called feminism a disease. When studying what happened, Microsoft claimed that their chatbot had been attacked by trolls, but the main problem was that the chatbot had simply been designed to trawl internet sites for plausible answers to questions. Lacking the ability to make judgements about the truth or otherwise of online abuse, the AI simply picked up the prejudices of the human contributors to these sites.[34]

To summarise, AIs will often generate far faster and more accurate data than is possible for human beings, and AI is not deliberately deceptive. Nevertheless, given the absence of the covenant of truth, which is implicit in most human interactions, AIs may also perfectly easily generate data that are plausibly accurate but wrong, or that lack judgements about truth. Similarly, AI can just as easily generate moral as immoral conclusions, provided the calculations are correct. Care is therefore needed to check that plausible and efficient AI outputs are also both true and good.

Conclusions

AI-related technologies can perform some tasks as well as or even better than human beings, and there are almost certainly going to be further impacts on employment and society. These impacts parallel those of the Industrial Revolution, when machines replaced much human labour. The difference is that AI machines will increasingly be able to perform some of the jobs traditionally associated with intellectual labour, at least in situations in which it is the product rather than the means of generation that matters. The transition to this state of liberty may be somewhat traumatic for individuals and societies, but AI-related technologies may also help liberate and vastly expand human discoveries, invention and creativity. These technologies can already be found across the Catholic world, from the digitised works of St Thomas Aquinas to the computer-aided designs for the *Sagrada Família* in Barcelona.

Most of the dangers surrounding AI are in fact ultimately due to the *absence* of capabilities associated with human intelligence, namely the absence of understanding, the absence of attention and free will, and the absence of a grasp of truth and goodness. We are understandably dazzled by the immense computational power of AI-related technologies, especially as they interface increasingly with human life and society. The danger is that we forget that these systems lack any appreciation of what is true and moral, especially as concerns the range of subgoals that a program can select to achieve an end. The failure in such instances, however, is ultimately due to a lack of human wisdom in neglecting to set proper safeguards. In other words, the real danger in AI is not machine intelligence but a failure to apply human intelligence. There is a parallel with the worship of idols by all kinds of people in the Old Testament, an idol being something that human beings create and then worship. Indeed, the author of one of the most famous books on AI-related issues introduces his text by stating explicitly "This book is a statement of my religion", consistent with the religious overtones that have often characterised this subject.[35] The problem, however, with turning to idols is that, as the Bible warns, "Their makers will be[come] like them" (*Ps* 115:8; 135:18). The fulfilment of this prophecy can be seen in the way in which unwise creators of AI, who turn their creations into idols, risk abdicating from the responsibilities of human intelligence. In Matthew 22:37-39, and elsewhere, Jesus Christ reminds us of the solution: "You shall love the Lord your God with all your heart, and with all your soul, and with all your mind" and "You shall love your neighbour as yourself". This perspective, in which we love the true God of love and respect the dignity of all persons, is in fact wholly compatible with the wise creation and use of AI.

Questions and Answers

Ethics of AI use

Q *I like to use AI to produce essays for my courses/reports for work. It's quicker and I don't have to work so hard at grammar and punctuation. Is there anything wrong with using AI to help me with writing?*

There are several reasons to be cautious about using AI to help with writing. First, in education and in many kinds of work, the purpose is not to generate essays but to develop intellectual skills. If the work of producing essays is outsourced to an AI, then the student does not benefit from the expenditure of money and time on the course. Second, AIs only produce plausible text rather than true text. Their outputs can often be riddled with errors and fake citations. Any information generated by an AI needs to be treated with care and independently verified wherever possible. Third, since AIs just try to predict new text based on existing text, they tend to plagiarise, which is a grave offence in academia and many professions.

Q *Isn't it a good thing if we can use AI to automate tasks that humans find especially time-consuming?*

As a rule, AI can almost certainly reduce the time and effort taken on many routine tasks. Automating repetitive tasks saves time and allows a more efficient allocation of human time and abilities. Nevertheless, care should still be taken to avoid missed opportunities, given that the acquisition of a great many human skills requires at least some repetitive and time-consuming work. For example, training a robot to play basketball or play the piano instead of training a human being means that the human being does not learn to play basketball or the piano.

Q *Are there morally good uses of programs like ChatGPT?*

Certainly, there are innumerable good uses for ChatGPT and similar programs, and more good uses are being invented with great frequency. These programs can be used as a fast and versatile (though not 100% accurate) way of searching for information found on the internet. They can be used to cheaply perform basic customer service. They can be used to quickly generate computer code, and in the slightly longer-term future, many routine jobs may be carried out by AI.

Q *Is it okay for me to tell chatbots personal details about myself and others?*

There are risks involved in putting personal or private information into an AI of any type. Often, this information is used to train the AI, so any information you share can become a part of what that program can use when generating material for someone else. Additionally, chatbots are sometimes monitored or reviewed by humans to scrutinise their performance, so there is no guarantee that what you type won't be read by another person. As with anything else involving the internet, never assume that what you type is secure or confidential, especially if you accepted the terms and conditions or privacy policies without reading them first.

Q *If I use AI to generate an image or text and use it verbatim for school or work, ethically speaking should I let people know it is AI generated?*

Yes, text or images that are AI-generated should be cited as such. There are many reasons for these citations. One is that they allow your readers to moderate their expectations about the output, namely that it does not represent your own thoughts and research but that it is the probabilistically generated result of an algorithm. Thus, they know that any claims in the texts or cited sources need to be independently verified. Another reason is that AIs have been known to copy text and images directly or with little modification without attribution, so citing the material as AI-generated offers a degree of protection against the accusation that one has plagiarised text deliberately.

Q *Is it safe for children to use AI, for example Snapchat's My AI?*

Using an AI is not inherently evil, and it can clearly be useful as a tool. Nevertheless, there are dangers for children using AI which are similar, but perhaps more subtle, than the dangers associated with their use of the internet. For example, an AI chatbot is an always accessible (and always dismissible) social substitute that may allow one to gain a semblance of a relationship without any of the commitment or suffering involved in a real relationship. As a result of an over-reliance on this substitute, children may fail to devote the time and energy needed to develop meaningful human relationships. Just as AI cannot have empathy, it doesn't require it and cannot effectively teach it, which means that children (or even adults) who spend more time interacting with AI than with other humans might not develop crucial social virtues like empathy, compromise, patience or kindness. Further, AIs do not push their users to refine their ideas or how they communicate: they will respond to virtually anything said, whether it is well thought-out and well articulated or not, which means that a reliance on AI for social interaction could also hamper cognitive development. Because a chatbot demands so little of its user, it can stifle ambition and perseverance simply through being too easy. As with so many other questions regarding AI, the dangers are much more to do with failures of human intelligence than machine malevolence. Despite the sacrifice of time and effort, parents will have to be astute to protect the souls of their children and to ensure that they, and not their machines, help form their minds.

Q *Is it morally acceptable to replace a human job with AI?*

Yes, it is acceptable to replace human jobs with AI as a special case of the more general moral permissibility of automation. For example, the goods produced by the AIs may be objectively better, and human beings may be liberated from labour that is not specifically human. Nevertheless, care is needed in overseeing such changes to protect human dignity and to avoid situations in which the loss of specifically human qualities would be damaging. For example, the replacement of human nurses with robotic nurses lacking judgement and empathy would be unacceptable.

AI, society and culture

Q *Could AI chatbots be a solution for loneliness and isolation?*

Chatbots are not a good solution for loneliness and isolation. They are incapable of actually understanding what a person says. They have no experience and cannot share attention with the person interacting with them. A sufficiently complex and well-trained AI might be able to create a convincing illusion of sharing awareness with a user, but even a convincing illusion of a relationship is still not a relationship.

Q *I am really worried about AI. Is it possible to not use it at all in my daily life?*

Some people working in certain kinds of jobs may use AI extensively. One of us, for example, spent years working in particle physics. Human beings, however, cannot study tens of thousands of particle collisions per second, so AI-type technology has been used for decades to filter automatically the very small percentage of collisions that might be of genuine interest for the advancement of physics. For most people, however, in most kinds of jobs, the impact of AI will most likely be commonplace but rather subtle for the immediate future. One example is the way in which the content of electronic messaging, including many social media interactions, is often prompted automatically by AIs. For example, when you hit 'reply' on an email, most platforms will immediately suggest a salutation and opening line. It is inevitable that this technology will become a part of modern life, just like other technological advances, such as moveable print, electric lights, microwave ovens and contactless payment. Caution with regard to some of the moral and privacy issues we have been discussing is warranted, but it is not necessary to reject AI technology because of these issues.

Q *Could an AI write a stand-up comedy routine that was both genuinely funny and original?*

Eventually, it may be possible for an AI to write or help write a comedy routine that is well received, but at present the best results still come from a human being working to optimise prompts to the AI and selecting those outputs that are worth keeping. Humour involves, among other things, a keen sense for the incongruities in human life and the ability to share this perception with one's audience. An AI might be able to identify patterns in the kinds of text that humans find humorous, but no system at the time of writing can actually participate in the experiences that humans find humorous.

Q *Of all the portrayals of AI in film and television, are there any that are especially realistic?*

As a rule, most portrayals of AI in film and television are completely unrealistic. As powerful as modern AI algorithms have become, they are still just pattern-matching engines. Large language models like ChatGPT, although they can appear humanlike, are really just very powerful autocomplete engines. These AIs are not in any way human and lack the capacity to act volitionally, but this truth is much less exciting than popular stories about godlike benevolent or malevolent machines. In fact, it is difficult to write an interesting story about AI without anthropomorphising the machine extensively, because the AI does not work as a character otherwise. For example, Commander Data from *Star Trek: The Next Generation* is a memorable and interesting character because he is portrayed as so nearly human, but the computer of the spacecraft is not thought of as a character per se, despite operating much like Alexa or Google Assistant.

Q *What are some big mistakes writers and filmmakers make in their portrayal of androids/AI/intelligent robots?*

Following on from the last question, in order to tell interesting stories, filmmakers often portray some fictional machines as personal, but these portrayals often have little to do with the actual nature or capabilities of machines. Further, filmmakers often do poorly in representing philosophical concepts such as personhood. To return to *Star Trek: The Next Generation*: the android Commander Data desires to gain human emotions, but the felt absence of emotions is itself an emotion, as is the curiosity that leads him to seek it. So it makes little sense for Data to say that he has no emotion. Filmmakers are in the business of telling fascinating stories, but their portrayals of AI generally have as little to do with actual computer science as *Pinocchio* has to do with actual puppet making.

AI and the Catholic faith

Q *Is it possible to teach an AI to say the Rosary for me? If I program it, does it count as praying?*

Actual prayer is a personal act whereby one addresses God and aligns with the will of God. This act requires the attention of one's mind, the focus of one's will, and somewhat secondarily, the alignment of one's emotions. This act is impossible for an AI, for all the reasons outlined in the main text. Moreover, a failure to do this act oneself would be detrimental to one's own spiritual health and flourishing, just as one cannot delegate the task of being a good friend to a machine. For all these reasons, an AI cannot pray as a substitute for one's own prayer.

Q *I think being able to talk to an AI rather than a priest would make many Catholics more likely to go to confession more often because they would be less embarrassed and they could confess ANY time. Could a priest teach a chatbot to hear confessions?*

For this question, we asked a new Catholic AI for an answer, and then assessed the quality of this answer as a test of the technology.[36]

The answer from an AI

According to the teachings of the Catholic Church, the sacrament of confession is a personal encounter between the penitent and the priest, who acts as a judge and a physician, ministering divine justice and mercy (*Code of Canon Law*, 1983, 978 §1). The priest is entrusted with the faculty to hear confessions, which is granted in writing (*Code of Canon Law*, 1983, 973). This faculty is given to bishops and cardinals by the law itself, allowing them to hear confessions everywhere unless it is denied by the diocesan bishop in a particular case (*Code of Canon Law*, 1983, 967 §1). The competent authority can grant the faculty to hear confessions for either an indefinite or a definite period of time (*Code of Canon Law*, 1983, 972).

Based on these teachings, it can be concluded that an AI cannot hear confession. The sacrament of confession requires the personal presence of a priest who has been granted the faculty to hear confessions. The priest's role as a judge and a physician, as well as the personal encounter between the penitent and the priest, are essential elements of the sacrament. An AI lacks the necessary faculties and personal presence to fulfil these requirements. Therefore, an AI cannot fulfil the role of a confessor in the sacrament of confession.

In conclusion, according to the teachings of the Catholic Church, an AI cannot hear confession because the sacrament requires the personal presence of a priest who has been granted the faculty to hear confessions (*Code of Canon Law*, 1983, 978 §1; 973; 967 §1; 972).

Evaluation of the AI's answer

The AI gave the correct conclusion, namely that an AI cannot hear confession. The AI also correctly highlighted the importance of the personal presence of a priest.

We would add a few further observations that are overlooked, however, in the answer. First, the sacrament is about restoring a relationship with God, with the priest acting in the person of Christ, and a machine cannot restore a relationship. Second, a machine cannot understand or actually empathise with a penitent, even though a well-programmed machine might generate appropriate questions and answers. Third, confidentiality must be assured for confession, which is conducted under a special seal of secrecy so that penitents are not prevented from confessing their sins for fear of publicity. Few, if any, such assurances of confidentiality can be given regarding AI or any kind of information technology.

We also note that the citations generated by this AI in response to this question are not quite correct, or not the best that could be cited. For example, the AI does not cite the Code of Canon Law, 1983, 965, "Only a priest is the minister of the sacrament of penance", or 970, "The faculty to hear confessions is not to be given except to priests whose suitability has been established, either by examination or by some other means." In addition, 968 §1 about bishops and parish priests, which the AI does not cite, would be more relevant than the more specialised canon 967 §1 about cardinals and bishops, which the AI does cite. This somewhat poor judgment about the choice of canons illustrates the difference between pattern matching done by an AI and the understanding of the human mind. This illustration also underlines the great care needed with AI-generated answers.

Q *Would it be better to use AI to pick a new pope than getting the cardinals to do it, since it reduces the likelihood of human prejudice?*

The answer is no, it would not be better to use an AI to pick a new pope, but there are some subtle points.

For example, there is one famous example in Scripture of impersonal means helping to select a bishop, namely the selection of St Matthias to replace Judas, who had betrayed Jesus. In this instance, the remaining apostles chose two candidates and then selected one of them by praying and then drawing lots (*Ac* 1:15-26). The problem with this example, however, is that the selection of St Matthias took place during a very short and unique time during the history of the Church, between the time of Jesus's Ascension and the Descent of the Holy Spirit, so it would be unwise to draw broader conclusions.

There are, indeed, many reasons for not using an AI. For example, it is unclear how a reward function would be specified for an AI to identify a good pope. As a famous example, none of the first apostles had many or indeed any suitable qualifications, and only one apostle, Judas the betrayer, had any influential connections in high places. The Church is much more like a garden than a machine, and the virtues of success are much more those of a gardener than a skilled manufacturer or machine-maker. Consistent with this understanding, the kinds of judgements needed to select bishops and popes require prudence and, ideally, openness to the promptings of the Holy Spirit, which is impossible for AIs.

Q *Can AIs be used to create authentic religious icons or devotional art?*

AIs may be of some assistance in creating icons or devotional art. For example, a human artist might use an AI to generate one or more initial images of, say, a woman holding her child. The artist could use this image as the basis for his or her own crafting of an image of the Madonna and Child. In such a case, the AI has not produced the final image but has only been a tool that contributed to the human's act of creation. Any attempt to create authentic religious icons or devotional art entirely by AI would be much more problematic. For instance, AIs cannot process many religious prompts accurately. One example noted previously is the prompt "Jesus flipping over tables" – a reference to his anger against the moneychangers in the Temple (*Mt* 21:12-17, *Mk* 11:15-19, *Lk* 19:45-48, *Jn* 2:13-16) – producing an image of Jesus performing a backwards somersault over the tables. Overall, the problems would at least be the same as all other such instances of AI-generated art, along with the problem that AIs cannot pray in the way that human artists of icons and devotional art pray to the Holy Spirit for inspiration. In conclusion, AIs would be of limited and partial use at best for this task.

Speculations and "what ifs" about AI

Q *Does AI think it's human? Does it want to be?*

A chatbot might output text that appears to claim that it is or wishes to be human or that it has human intelligence, but only because its model predicts a text string such as "Are you human?" is likely to be followed by a text string such as "Yes, I am". This answer is consistent with a huge body of fiction in which nonhumans (many of them specifically robots or computers in science fiction) claim to be or to aspire to be human. For all the reasons stated in the main text, however, no AI thinks it is human; nor can any AI want to be human, or be said to want anything at all.

Q *Could AI decide to harm humans?*

In the strict sense, an AI cannot decide to harm humans. An AI could, however, be designed, by commission or omission, to act in a way that does cause harm. This fact is already true of weapons that are, to some degree, autonomous. A guided missile, for instance, makes calculations to ensure that its target is destroyed. It is likely that future weapon systems will be designed that include AI, say in a drone that makes tactical calculations about how to strike assigned targets. Alternatively, AI might be used to try to identify enemy combatants in a crowd, information that might be fed either to human soldiers or to automated weaponry. It is also at least possible that an AI with control of real-world systems might be designed with a reward function that, unintentionally, causes it to act in a way that harms humans. As noted in the main text, the problems in these unintended cases are due not to the malevolence of AI but to a failure of human intelligence.

Q *If a government decided to turn off all the AI, would AI allow itself to be turned off? Would it 'fight back'?*

There is no definitive answer to this question since any answer depends on the characteristics of the system under consideration. At time of writing, every extant AI system could, in principle, be turned off without opposition from the system, so the concern is about hypothetical future systems with greater capabilities than currently exist. AI systems do not have a sense of self-preservation in the sense that humans do, but they do try to find optimal solutions to the problem they have been set. One hypothesis is that an AI might discover that to pursue some solution it needs to prevent itself from being turned off or otherwise thwarted in pursuing that goal. Hence, the AI might fight back against attempts to shut it down. Nevertheless, as noted previously, these problems would not be due to the malevolence of AI, but rather to a failure of human intelligence.

Q *Could multiple AIs ever have conflicts, or even wars, which had nothing to do with humans?*

In a sense, multiple AIs can have conflicts, for they can already be in competition. Examples of deliberately created competition between AIs include OpenAI's hide and seek simulation.[37] It is likely that, as AIs are increasingly deployed in the world, they will deliberately be placed in competition with each other by humans, say in managing the investments of competing financial firms. Whether or not any AI systems that will be deployed will end up entering into competition with one another unexpectedly is unknown, but it does not appear impossible. The broader question of whether or not wars could be initiated and fought by AIs with complete independence from human beings depends, further, on whether or not war can be fully automated, which is certainly impossible at present.

Bibliography

Bostrom, Nick. "Ethical Issues in Advanced Artificial Intelligence". In *Cognitive, Emotive and Ethical Aspects of Decision Making in Humans and in Artificial Intelligence*, edited by I. Smit, 1st ed., 2:12-17. Int. Institute of Advanced Studies in Systems Research and Cybernetics, 2003.

Dreyfus, Hubert L. *What Computers Still Can't Do: A Critique of Artificial Reason*. Cambridge, MA: MIT Press, 1992.

Future of Life Institute. "Pause Giant AI Experiments: An Open Letter". Accessed 12th October 2023. *https://futureoflife. org/open-letter/pause-giant-ai-experiments/*.

Hofstadter, Douglas. *Godel, Escher, Bach: An Eternal Golden Braid*. 20th Anniversary ed. New York: Basic Books, 1999.

Jones, Alexander. *Portable Cosmos: Revealing the Antikythera Mechanism, Scientific Wonder of the Ancient World*. Illustrated edition. New York, NY: Oxford University Press, 2017.

Jones, Steven E. *Roberto Busa, S.J., and the Emergence of Humanities Computing: The Priest and the Punched Cards*. 1st edition. New York; London: Routledge, 2018.

Lehman, J., J. Clune, D. Misevic, C. Adami, L. Altenberg, J. Beaulieu, P. J. Bentley, et al. "The Surprising Creativity of Digital Evolution: A Collection of Anecdotes from the Evolutionary Computation and Artificial Life Research Communities". *Artificial Life* (2020) 26 (2). *https://doi.org/10. 1162/artl_a_00319*.

Literaturwelt.com, "Der Zauberlehrling – Johann Wolfgang von Goethe", 19th June 2021. *https://www.literaturwelt.com/ der-zauberlehrling-von-goethe/*.

Magisterium.com, "Magisterium AI". Accessed 20th October 2023. *www.magisterium.com*.

Mason, Paul. "The Racist Hijacking of Microsoft's Chatbot Shows How the Internet Teems with Hate". *The Guardian*, 29th March 2016.

McGilchrist, Iain. *The Master and His Emissary: The Divided Brain and the Making of the Western World*. 2nd edition. New Haven: Yale University Press, 2019.

McKeown, Jonah. "Here's What the Catholic Church Says about Artificial Intelligence", 15th June 2022. *https://www.catholic newsagency.com/news/251552/sentient-ai-heres-what-the-catholic-church-says-about-artificial-intelligence*.

Office of National Statistics. "Fall in HGV Drivers Largest among Middle-Aged Workers", 19th October 2021. *https:// www.ons.gov.uk/employmentandlabourmarket/peoplein work/employmentandemployeetypes/articles/fallinhgvdrivers largestamongmiddleagedworkers/2021-10-19*.

Omolesky, Matthew. "The Painter and the Chatbot: Artificial Intelligence and the Perils of Progress". *The American Spectator*, 7th July 2023.

OpenAI. "Emergent Tool Use from Multi-Agent Interaction". Accessed 22nd October 2023. *https://openai.com/research/ emergent-tool-use*.

OpenAI. "GPT-4 Technical Report". arXiv.Org, 2023. *https:// doi.org/10.48550/arxiv.2303.08774*.

OpenAI. "Learning from Human Preferences". Accessed 20th October 2023. *https://openai.com/research/learning-from-human-preferences*.

Oxford University Press. "Artificial Intelligence, n.". *Oxford English Dictionary*. Accessed October 12, 2023. *https://www.oed.com/dictionary/artificial-intelligence_n?tab=meaning_and_use#38531565*.

Pinsent, Andrew. *The Second-Person Perspective in Aquinas's Ethics: Virtues and Gifts*. New York; Abingdon, UK: Routledge, 2012.

Pontifical Academy for Life. "Artificial Intelligence" 2020. Accessed 22nd October 2023. *https://www.academyforlife.va/content/pav/en/projects/artificial-intelligence.html*.

Raczynski, Joseph. "Possible End of Humanity from AI? Geoffrey Hinton at MIT Technology Review's EmTech Digital, 2023". YouTube video. 4th May 2023. *https://www.youtube.com/watch?v=sitHS6UDMJc*.

Sadler, Matthew, Natasha Regan, Garry Kasparov, and Demis Hassabis. *Game Changer: AlphaZero's Groundbreaking Chess Strategies and the Promise of AI*. New In Chess, 2019.

Searle, John. "Minds, Brains and Programs". *Behavioral and Brain Sciences* 3, no. 3 (1980): 417-57.

Swinbanks, David, and Christopher Anderson. "Japan Stubs Its Toes on Fifth-Generation Computer". *Nature* 356 (26th March 1992): 273-74.

Tallis, Raymond. *Seeing Ourselves: Reclaiming Humanity from God and Science*. Newcastle upon Tyne: Agenda Publishing, 2019.

Toole, Betty A. *Ada: The Enchantress of Numbers*. Strawberry Press, 1998.

Turing, Alan. "Computing Machinery and Intelligence". *Mind* LIX, no. 236 (n.d.): 433-60. *https://doi.org/10.1093/mind/LIX.236.433*.

Turkle, Sherry. "Empathy Machines: Forgetting the Body". In *A Psychoanalytic Exploration of the Body in Today's World: On the Body*, edited by Vaia Tsolas and Christine Anzieu-Premmereur, 1st ed., 17-27. Routledge, 2017.

Weiser, Benjamin, and Nate Schweber. "The Lawyer Who Relied on ChatGPT Explains Himself. It Was Awkward". *The New York Times*, 9th June 2023, sec. B.

Weizenbaum, Joseph. *Computer Power and Human Reason: From Judgment to Calculation*. Harmondsworth: Penguin, 1984.

Endnotes

[1] Jonah McKeown, "Here's What the Catholic Church Says about Artificial Intelligence", 15th June 2022, *https://www.catholicnewsagency.com/news/251552/sentient-ai-heres-what-the-catholic-church-says-about-artificial-intelligence*.

[2] Pontifical Academy for Life, "Artificial Intelligence", 2020, *https://www.academyforlife.va/content/pav/en/projects/artificial-intelligence.html; https://www.romecall.org/*.

[3] Oxford University Press, "Artificial Intelligence, n.", *Oxford English Dictionary*, accessed 12th October 2023, *https://www.oed.com/dictionary/artificial-intelligence_n?tab=meaning_and_use#38531565*.

[4] Alexander Jones, *Portable Cosmos: Revealing the Antikythera Mechanism, Scientific Wonder of the Ancient World*, Illustrated edition (New York, NY: Oxford University Press, 2017).

5   Betty A. Toole, *Ada, the Enchantress of Numbers: Prophet of the Computer Age* (Strawberry Press, 1998) 38. Italics have been added along with minor changes to the form of the words.

6   "Fall in HGV Drivers Largest among Middle-Aged Workers", Office of National Statistics (blog), October 19, 2021, *https://www.ons.gov.uk/employmentandlabourmarketpeoplein workemploymentandemployeetypesarticles/fallinhgv driverslargestamongmiddleagedworkers/2021-10-19*.

7   Steven E. Jones, *Roberto Busa, S.J., and the Emergence of Humanities Computing: The Priest and the Punched Cards* (New York: Routledge, 2016).

8   "Midjourney v6: The Next Leap in AI Art Generation", 21st September 2023, *https://mid-journey.ai/midjourney-v6/*.

9   Matthew Omolesky, "The Painter and the Chatbot: Artificial Intelligence and the Perils of Progress", *The American Spectator*, 7th July 2023, para. 5.

10   *Mt* 21:12-17; *Mk* 11:15-19; *Lk* 19:45-48 and *Jn* 2:13-16.

11   We are grateful to Victoria Seed for pointing out this example.

12   Matthew Sadler et al., *Game Changer: AlphaZero's Groundbreaking Chess Strategies and the Promise of AI* (Netherlands: New in Chess, 2019) 62.

13   "Der Zauberlehrling – Johann Wolfgang von Goethe", 19th June 2021, *https://www.literaturwelt.com/der-zauberlehrling -von-goethe/*.

14   David Swinbanks and Christopher Anderson, "Japan Stubs Its Toes on Fifth-Generation Computer", *Nature* 356 (1992): 273-74.

15   *Possible End of Humanity from AI? Geoffrey Hinton at MIT Technology Review's EmTech Digital*, 2023, *https://www. youtube.com/watch?v=sitHS6UDMJc*.

[16] Future of Life Institute, "Pause Giant AI Experiments: An Open Letter" (blog), accessed 12th October 2023, *https:// futureoflife.org/open-letter/pause-giant-ai-experiments/*.

[17] Nick Bostrom, "Ethical Issues in Advanced Artificial Intelligence", in *Cognitive, Emotive and Ethical Aspects of Decision Making in Humans and in Artificial Intelligence*, ed. I. Smit, 1st ed., vol. 2 (Int. Institute of Advanced Studies in Systems Research and Cybernetics, 2003) 12-17.

[18] *Possible End of Humanity from AI?*

[19] OpenAI, "GPT-4 Technical Report" in arXiv.Org, 2023, 55, *https://doi.org/10.48550/arxiv.2303.08774*.

[20] *Possible End of Humanity from AI?*

[21] For example, some AIs change behaviour when they are observed. See J. Lehman et al., "The Surprising Creativity of Digital Evolution: A Collection of Anecdotes from the Evolutionary Computation and Artificial Life Research Communities", *Artificial Life* (2020) 26 (2): 282, *https://doi.org/10.1162/artl_a_00319*. Another AI tricked the human observer into thinking that it had actually performed some task. See OpenAI, "Learning from Human Preferences", accessed 20th October 2023, *https://openai.com/research/learning-from-human-preferences*.

[22] Voltaire, *Oeuvres Complètes de Voltaire* (Paris: P. Plancher, 1819) 491.

[23] The example of climbing a tree to get closer to the moon comes from the conclusion of Hubert L Dreyfus, *What Computers Still Can't Do: A Critique of Artificial Reason* (Cambridge, MA: MIT Press, 1992).

[24] Joseph Weizenbaum, *Computer Power and Human Reason: From Judgment to Calculation* (Harmondsworth: Penguin, 1984), 189.

[25] Weizenbaum, 5-6.

[26] Weizenbaum, 7-8.

[27] Iain McGilchrist, *The Master and His Emissary: The Divided Brain and the Making of the Western World*, 2nd edition (New Haven: Yale University Press, 2019).

[28] Alan Turing, "Computing Machinery and Intelligence", Mind LIX, no. 236 (n.d.): 433-60, *https://doi.org/10.1093/mind/LIX.236.433*.

[29] John Searle, "Minds, Brains and Programs", *Behavioral and Brain Sciences* 3, no. 3 (1980): 417-57.

[30] Raymond Tallis, *Seeing Ourselves: Reclaiming Humanity from God and Science* (Newcastle upon Tyne: Agenda Publishing, 2019) 49-60.

[31] Andrew Pinsent, *The Second-Person Perspective in Aquinas's Ethics: Virtues and Gifts* (New York; Abingdon, UK: Routledge, 2012).

[32] Benjamin Weiser and Nate Schweber, "The Lawyer Who Relied on ChatGPT Explains Himself. It Was Awkward", *The New York Times*, 9th June 2023, sec. B.

[33] Indeed, it may be technically impossible to eliminate the tendency of large language models to create believable confabulations. The designers are aware that, paradoxically, the danger of plausible but false answers being accepted increases as the AI becomes more truthful in its answers, because users become more likely to trust answers will be not only plausible but correct despite the certainty that some percentage of the time the answers will be untrue. OpenAI, "GPT-4 Technical Report": 46.

[34] Paul Mason, "The Racist Hijacking of Microsoft's Chatbot Shows How the Internet Teems with Hate" *The Guardian*, 29th March 2016.

[35] Douglas Hofstadter, *Gödel, Escher, Bach: An Eternal Golden Braid*, 20th Anniversary edition (New York: Basic Books, 1999) xxi.

[36] "Magisterium AI", accessed 20th October 2023, *www. magisterium.com*. Note that the website adds the sensible warning "Magisterium AI is in beta and trained on a limited, but growing number of Magisterial documents. Its responses are not always perfect. When in doubt consult a human."

[37] OpenAI, "Emergent Tool Use from Multi-Agent Interaction", accessed 22nd October 2023, *https://openai.com/research/ emergent-tool-use*.